Praise for [illegible] and H[illegible]

"I am always looking for ideas that help people enrich their lives. This book does just that. I highly recommend you read it...it will feed your soul, life your spirits, and help you live a fuller, richer, and more joy-filled life."

—SARK (Susan Ariel Rainbow Kennedy), author of *Juicy Living*

"Allen Klein is a noble and vital force watching over the human condition."

—Jerry Lewis, actor/comedian

"I have come to know that sometimes the simplest words can make a major difference in how people perceive and interact with their world. This book can make that same difference to you."

—Jack Canfield, coauthor of *Chicken Soup for the Soul*

"Allen Klein's purpose is to make us feel inspired again, to bask in laughter and revel in joy."

—*OMTimes*

"A wonderful collection of timeless inspiration and powerful insights."

—Randy Gage, author of *Prosperity Mind*

"This powerful collection of quotes serves as a great reminder of simple truths and timeless wisdom that can alter our lives in a profound way. This book is guaranteed to inspire all who read it."

—Mike Robbins, author of *Focus on the Good Stuff*

"This book will wake you up and show you how this day may truly be the best day of your life."

—Kristine Carlson, coauthor of the Don't Sweat the Small Stuff series

"Allen's writing will lift your spirit and inspire you."

—Gloria Horsley, president and cofounder of Open to Hope

"Quotes ARE fuel for the soul, and Allen has packed enough fuel in this book to shine a light of positivity and hope that will glow for eternity."

—G. Brian Benson, author of *Habits for Success*

"Let Allen Klein inspire you and help you embrace and celebrate the joy in your life and in the life that surrounds you."

—Carole Brody Fleet, author of *Happily Ever After*

The Joy of Simplicity

Also by Allen Klein:

The Lighten Up Book

Positive Thoughts for Troubling Times

Embracing Life After Loss

You Can't Ruin My Day

Secrets Kids Know...That Adults Oughta Learn

Change Your Life! A Little Book of Big Ideas

Having the Time of Your Life

The Art of Living Joyfully

Always Look on the Bright Side

Words of Love

Mom's the Word

Inspiration for a Lifetime

The Courage to Laugh

The Healing Power of Humor

Learning to Laugh When You Feel Like Crying

L.A.U.G.H.: Using Humor and Play to Help Clients Cope

The Joy of Simplicity

ALLEN KLEIN

Bestselling author of
The Healing Power of Humor

Foreword by David Kundtz, S.Th.D.
Bestselling author of
Quiet Mind: One Minute Mindfulness

mango
PUBLISHING
CORAL GABLES

Published by Mango Publishing Group, a division of Mango Media Inc.

Cover, Layout & Design: Morgane Leoni

For permission requests, please contact the publisher at:
Mango Publishing Group
2850 S Douglas Road, 2nd Floor
Coral Gables, FL 33134 USA
info@mango.bz

For special orders, quantity sales, course adoptions and corporate sales, please email the publisher at sales@mango.bz. For trade and wholesale sales, please contact Ingram Publisher Services at customer.service@ingramcontent.com or +1.800.509.4887.

The Joy of Simplicity: Insights to Unclutter and Uncomplicate Your Life

Library of Congress Cataloging-in-Publication number: 2019948829
ISBN: (print) 978-1-64250-145-2, (ebook) 978-1-64250-146-9
BISAC category code REF019000, REFERENCE / Quotations

Printed in the United States of America

For my friends Kevin and Will,
whose lives were simple, yet rich.

Our life is frittered away by detail...
simplify, simplify.

Henry David Thoreau

Contents

Foreword

I was particularly pleased when Allen asked me to write the foreword for *The Joy of Simplicity* because the subject matter is closely related to the books I have written. While we each take a different approach to writing, we are both on a path to help readers live a simpler, more mindful, and joyful life. What is so wonderful about this book is that Allen does so in an easy-to-read, readily digestible format.

I think you would agree with me that there is truly an enormous amount of wisdom available to people today. For the first time in human experience we can, with relative ease, access practically all the accumulated knowledge in the history of humankind. That's the good news. The bad? Who has the time–or even the inclination and skills–to go in search of it?

That's where Allen Klein comes in; he's done so much of the work for us.

Allen's considerable talents and training in the arts and communications make him the perfect researcher of wisdom–especially the practical kind that gives you help and insight into the ins and outs of today's challenges of living, as the subtitle says, an uncluttered and uncomplicated life. This is so because he recognizes the salient and the noble and can distinguish those categories from the ephemeral and misleading. He has the rare talent that clearly separates the wheat from the chaff.

In addition, he has organized this wisdom into convenient categories that will help you in your own search for living a simpler more satisfying life.

So, whether you decide to read it from beginning to end, enjoy one gem per day, or simply open at random and see what you get, you'll always come away saying, "Thanks, Allen!"

—David Kundtz, S.Th.D.,
author of the bestseller *Quiet Mind: One Minute Mindfulness*

Introduction

While writing this book, I was extremely busy. My speaking schedule was full, I was working on several other projects, and I was about to become the president of the Association for Applied and Therapeutic Humor. Here I was, compiling information about how to make your life simpler and mine was getting more complicated every day.

Then I started to take the advice of the quotations I was gathering. What I found was that their words helped me slow down, prioritize what was most important, and actually get more done in a calmer, more relaxed frame of mind.

It has been said that we teach what we need to learn. Obviously, I needed to hear about the wisdom of simplicity. I learned a lot from this book. I hope you do too.

Allen Klein
San Francisco, CA
www.allenklein.com

Be Present

The only thing we really have is the present. It has been said that yesterday is gone and tomorrow isn't here yet. Many of us don't acknowledge that. We obsess over things that happened a long time ago. Or we fantasize about what might happen in the future.

Part of the problem of being present is that our world is overcrowded with things that distract us from being in the moment. We are inundated with emails, phone calls, and text messages, along with social media such as Facebook, Twitter, Instagram, etc.

At work or at home, we are often multitasking. No wonder many of us stress out. We are asking our minds and bodies to do several things at once. And it just doesn't work well. It not only is inefficient, but it also robs us of fully enjoying what is before us.

The quotation in this section by the Vietnamese monk Thich Nhat Hanh is perhaps the best advice we can have about being present. What he says is, when you wash dishes, wash dishes. In other words, feel the warm water, see the bubbling soap suds, smell the dishwashing liquid, and stop thinking about what happened at work today or what we will do after the dishes are done.

Along with that inspiring quotation, there are many more here to gently remind us about the importance of living in the moment.

Paradise is where I am.

Voltaire

One of the ultimate objectives of attaining inner simplicity is to learn to live happily in the present moment.

Elaine St. James

We do not remember days, we remember moments.

Cesare Pavese

Life is a succession of moments. To live each one is to succeed.

Corita Kent

The more I give myself permission to live in the moment and enjoy it without feeling guilty or judgmental about any other time, the better I feel about the quality of my work.

Wayne Dyer

Living in the moment means letting go of the past and not waiting for the future. It means living your life consciously, aware that each moment you breathe is a gift.

Oprah Winfrey

Make it a rule of life never to regret and never to look back.
Regret is an appalling waste of energy; you can't build on it;
it's only good for wallowing in.

Katherine Mansfield

It is only possible to live happily ever after
on a day-to-day basis.

Margaret Bonnano

Reflect upon your present blessings, of which
every man has many—not on your past misfortunes,
of which all men have some.

Charles Dickens

Look to this day! For it is life, the very life of life.

Kalidasa

To live is so startling, it leaves little time for anything else.

Emily Dickinson

It's not that "today is the first day of the rest of your life,"
but that now is all there is of my life.

Hugh Prather

How we spend our days is, of course, how we spend our lives.

Annie Dillard

The ideal day never comes.
Today is ideal for him who makes it so.

Horatio Dresser

If we are ever to enjoy life, now is the time....
Today should always be our most wonderful day.

Thomas Dreier

Only that day dawns to which we are awake.

Henry David Thoreau

It's only when we truly know and understand that we have a limited time on earth—and that we have no way of knowing when our time is up—that we will begin to live each day to the fullest, as if it was the only one we had.

Elisabeth Kübler-Ross

May you live every day of your life.

Jonathan Swift

There is only one world, the world pressing against you
at this minute. There is only one minute in which you are alive,
this minute here and now. The only way to live is by
accepting each minute as an unrepeatable miracle.

Storm Jameson

Every day we are engaged in a miracle which we don't even
recognize: a blue sky, white clouds, green leaves, the black,
curious eyes of a child—our own two eyes. All is a miracle.

Thich Nhat Hanh

Today a new sunrise for me; everything lives,
everything is animated, everything seems to speak to me
of my passion, everything invites me to cherish it.

Anne de Lenclos

The moment one gives close attention to anything,
even a blade of grass, it becomes a mysterious, awesome,
indescribably magnificent world in itself.

Henry Miller

Finally it has penetrated my thick skull.
This life—this moment—is no dress rehearsal. This is it!

Fletcher Knebel

"Now thyself" is more important than "Know thyself."
Reason is what tells us to ignore the
present and live in the future.
So all we do is make plans. We think that somewhere there are
going to be green pastures. It's crazy. Heaven is nothing
but a grand, monumental instance of future.
Listen, now is good. Now is wonderful.

Mel Brooks

The experience of eternity right here
and now is the function of life.
Heaven is not the place to have the experience;
here's the place to have the experience.

Joseph Campbell

These are the good old days.

Anonymous

Do not look back on happiness, or dream of it in the future.
You are only sure of today; do not let
yourself be cheated out of it.

Henry Ward Beecher

The present moment is significant, not as the bridge between past and future, but by reason of its contents, which can fill our emptiness and become ours, if we are capable of receiving them.

Dag Hammarskjöld

Accept yourself, your physical condition, and your fate as they are at the present moment.

Morrie Schwartz

Love the moment, and the energy of the moment will spread beyond all boundaries.

Corita Kent

Do what you can, with what you have, where you are.

Theodore Roosevelt

When you stop comparing what is right here and now with what you wish were, you can begin to enjoy what is.

Cheri Huber

Spend the afternoon. You can't take it with you.

Annie Dillard

The secret of health for both mind and body is
not to mourn for the past, nor to worry about the future,
but to live the present moment wisely and earnestly.

Buddha

The present contains all that there is.
It is holy ground, for it is the past, and it is the future.

Alfred North Whitehead

The art of life is to live in the present moment, and to make that
moment as perfect as we can by the realization that we are
the instruments and expression of God Himself.

Emmet Fox

If I am incapable of washing dishes joyfully, if I want
to finish them quickly so I can go and have dessert,
I will be equally incapable of enjoying my dessert.
With the fork in hand, I will be thinking about
what to do next, and the texture and flavor of the
dessert, together with the pleasure of eating it, will
be lost. I will always be dragged into the future,
never able to live in the present moment.

Thich Nhat Hanh

You don't own the future, you don't own the past.
Today is all you have.

Les Brown

You can clutch the past so tightly to
your chest that it leaves your
arms too full to embrace the present.

Jan Glidewell

The past exists only in our memories,
the future only in our plans.
The present is our only reality.

Robert Pirsig

It is difficult to live in the present, ridiculous to live
in the future, and impossible to live in the past.
Nothing is as far away as one minute ago.

Jim Bishop

I live now and only now, and I will do what I want to do this
moment and not what I decided was best for me yesterday.

Hugh Prather

Don't make the mistake of letting yesterday
use up too much of today.

Anonymous

Do not boast about tomorrow, for
you do not know what a day may bring forth.

Proverbs 27:1

One today is worth two tomorrows.

Benjamin Franklin

Leave tomorrow until tomorrow.

German proverb

The best thing about the future
is that it comes only one day at a time.

Abraham Lincoln

Do Less

The blurb under my high school yearbook photo read, "Ambition has no rest."

Is it no wonder then that every day I have a very long to-do list? And is it no surprise then that, at the end of every day, I get frustrated when I view that list and find that I haven't accomplished half of what I set out to do?

Perhaps you have found yourself in the same situation. Well, here is a solution that I just learned from listening to a podcast from Tim Ferriss, author of *The 4-Hour Workweek*. Although he was discussing procrastination, I realized that his remarks were applicable to doing less.

According to Ferriss, I need to rethink my daily to-do list. Instead of trying to accomplish everything on it, which is overwhelming, one of the things he suggests is lowering our expectations. If one of the tasks on the list is large, break it down into very small, doable items. Or, take the long list and reduce it down to a few manageable items. By doing that, you will get a sense of accomplishment that will help spur you on to your next thing on the list.

In other words, by doing less, as a number of quotations in the following section remind us, you might actually accomplish more.

Besides the noble art of getting things done,
there is the noble art of leaving things undone.
The wisdom of life consists in the elimination of non-essentials.

Lin Yutang

The great secret of life [is] not to open
your letters for a fortnight.
At the expiration of that period you will
find that nearly all of them
have answered themselves.

Arthur Binstead

Throw out the excess, clean up the mess,
say no to stress, and live with less.

Joshua Becker

Don't answer the phone just because it's ringing.

Elaine St. James

If someone throws you the ball, you don't have to catch it.

Richard Carlson

There is one piece of advice, in a life of study,
which I think no one will object to; and that is,
every now and then to be completely idle—do nothing at all.

Sydney Smith

The Master arrives without leaving,
sees the light without looking,
achieves without doing a thing.

Lao-Tzu

If it's working, keep doing it.
If it's not working, stop doing it.
If you don't know what to do, don't do anything.

Melvin Konner

To do great work, a man must be very idle
as well as very industrious.

Samuel Butler

He lacks much who has no aptitude for idleness.

Louise Beebe Wilder

He does not seem to me to be a free man
who does not sometimes do nothing.

Cicero

It's not enough to be busy.... The question is:
What are we busy about?

Henry David Thoreau

The Chinese word for "busy" consists of two parts.
One part symbolizes the human heart, the other part
symbolizes death. The meaning that can be extrapolated
is that when one is excessively busy, his heart is dead.

Chin-Ning Chu

I have a very full and busy life and
occasionally am asked, "Scotty,
how can you do all that you do?" There are multiple answers...
but the most telling reply I can give is:
"Because I spend at least two
hours a day doing nothing." Ironically, the questioner usually
responds by saying he's too busy to do that.

M. Scott Peck

To do nothing is in every man's power.

Samuel Johnson

Each week, watch one fewer hour-long television show.

Jeff Davidson

You have to allow a certain amount of
time in which you are doing
nothing in order to have things occur to
you, to let your mind think.

Mortimer Adler

To do nothing is sometimes a good remedy.

Hippocrates

Guard the senses and life is ever full...
always be busy and life is beyond hope.

Lao-Tzu

If you can spend a perfectly useless afternoon in a perfectly useless manner, you have learned how to live.

Lin Yutang

Never again clutter your days or nights with so many menial and unimportant things that you have no time to accept a real challenge when it comes along.... No more busy work.... Leave time, leave space, to grow.

Og Mandino

Leisure and cultivation of human capacities are inextricably interdependent.

Margaret Mead

A broad margin of leisure is as beautiful in a man's life as in a book. Haste makes waste, no less in life than in housekeeping. Keep the time, observe the hours of the universe, not of the cars.

Henry David Thoreau

Take time to come home to yourself every day.

Robin Casarjian

Guard well your spare moments. They are like uncut diamonds.

Ralph Waldo Emerson

I would not exchange my leisure hours
for all the wealth in the world.

Comte de Mirabeau

It's not easy saying no. We're so used to thinking we should
be able to taste every darned thing on the banquet table
that we wind up not enjoying any of it.

Janet Luhrs

No one can maintain more than three priorities....
Figure out what your priorities are, and
say no to everything else.

Elaine St. James

Tell him to live by yes and no—
yes to everything good, no to everything bad.

William James

There is no pleasure in having nothing to do;
the fun is in having lots to do—and not doing it.

Mary Wilson Little

I've learned that you can't have everything
and do everything at the same time.

Oprah Winfrey

To do two things at once is to do neither.

Publilius Syrus

Trying to remember too many things is certainly one of
the major sources of psychologic stress. I make a conscious
effort to forget immediately all that is unimportant
and to jot down data of possible value.

Hans Selye

Always do one thing less than you think you can do.

Bernard Baruch

Less is more.

Ludwig Mies van der Rohe

Focus on What's Important

One of my friends coauthored a wonderful book titled *Living Your Life Out Loud*. While the book's main focus was to help readers unlock their creativity, it contained a few sentences that opened my eyes to how much time I waste on unimportant activities. I've included that quotation in this section, but because it is so valuable, it is worth repeating:

> "We all have 100 percent to deal with in our lives: 10 percent is important, 90 percent unimportant. The secret to a happy, productive life is to deal with the 10 percent and let the 90 percent slip."

What the authors are emphasizing is the importance of setting priorities. Just because someone does something or asks you to do something doesn't mean you have to do it. Saying "no" is perhaps the most valuable skill you can use to focus on, and accomplish, what you want to achieve.

When I was writing my first book, *The Healing Power of Humor*, I had a deadline to complete the manuscript in nine months. I was under contract to write 120,000 words. I had never written a book before, so I had no idea how long this daunting task would take. I was afraid of missing the deadline, so I said "no" to anything that would take time away from my writing.

It annoyed some of my friends, who accused me of neglecting them, but writing and finishing the book was important to me.

Because I focused on what needed to get done, I did meet the deadline. The book, I'm happy to say, is now in its fortieth-plus printing with nine foreign language translations.

P.S. And, even though it was many years ago, my friends are still talking to me.

Often, people attempt to live their lives backwards:
they try to have more things, or more money, in order to
do more of what they want so that they will be happier.
The way it actually works is the reserve. You must first
be who you really are, then, do what you need to do,
in order to have what you want.

Margaret Young

What really matters is what you do with what you have.

Shirley Lord

You have to accept whatever comes, and
the only important thing is
that you meet it with the best you have to give.

Eleanor Roosevelt

The great opportunity is where you are. Do not despise
your own place and hour. Every place is under the stars,
every place is the center of the world.

John Burroughs

I always say to myself, what is the most important thing
we can think about at this extraordinary moment?

François de La Rochefoucauld

The best things in life are the nearest: breath in your nostrils,
light in your eyes, flowers at your feet, duties at your hand,
the path of right just before you.

Robert Louis Stevenson

You're only here for a short visit. Don't hurry, don't worry.
And be sure to smell the flowers along the way.

Walter Hagen

In hope of reaching the moon, men fail to see the flowers
that blossom at their feet.

Albert Schweitzer

Millions of persons long for immortality who do not know
what to do with themselves on a rainy afternoon.

Susan Ertz

To find the universal elements enough; to find the air and the
water exhilarating; to be refreshed by a morning walk
or an evening saunter...to be thrilled by the stars at night;
to be elated over a bird's nest or a wildflower in spring
—these are some of the rewards of a simple life.

John Burroughs

If you wish to know the divine,
feel the wind on your face and the warm sun on your hand.

Buddha

Get pleasure out of your life...as much as you can.
Nobody ever died from pleasure.

Sol Hurok

If you break your neck, if you have nothing to eat,
if your house is on fire—then you got a problem.
Everything else is inconvenience.

Robert Fulghum

One way to high blood pressure
is to go mountain climbing over molehills.

Earl Wilson

Get your priorities straight. Looking
back, no one ever wished that
he or she had returned more phone calls
or attended more meetings.

Odette Pollar

Why not spend more time in determining
what is worthwhile for us, and then go after that?

William Ross

If I die tomorrow,
I hope I've spent this day doing what I truly want to do and not
picking up the dry cleaning and going
to the salmon sale at Safeway.

Lynn Befera

I have only one life and it is short enough.
Why waste it on things I don't want most?

Louis Brandeis

You decide what it is you want to accomplish
and then you lay out your plans to get there,
and then you just do it. It's pretty straightforward.

Nancy Ditz

Live your life each day as you would climb a mountain.
An occasional glance toward the summit
keeps the goal in mind,
but many beautiful scenes are to be observed
from each new vantage point.

Harold B. Melchart

What is the center of your life? Carefully
examine where you spend
your attention, your time. Look at your appointment book, your
daily schedule...This is what receives your care and attention—
and, by definition, your love.

Wayne Muller

I was rich, if not in money, in sunny hours and summer days,
and spent them lavishly.

Henry David Thoreau

I don't think God puts you on this earth just to make millions of
dollars and ignore everything else.

Chris Amundsen

Keep your job and your life in perspective.
Success at the expense of relaxation
and enjoyment is no success.

Odette Pollar

It's not the honors and the prizes and the fancy outsides of life
that ultimately nourish our souls. It's the knowing
that we can be trusted, that we never have to fear the truth,
that the bedrock of our very being is firm.

Fred Rogers

Know what's important to you. Ask yourself what really matters
in your relationships, your work, and for you individually.
Then ask yourself: "Do I spend my time
on things that really matter
to me? Or do I spend my time on other people's goals?"

Daniel Amen

Don't let other people tell you what you want.

Pat Riley

Time is the coin of your life. It is the only coin you have,
and only you can determine how it will be spent.
Be careful lest you let other people spend it for you.

Carl Sandburg

I am thankful for small mercies. I compared notes with one
of my friends who expects everything of the universe and is
disappointed when anything is less than the best, and I found
that I begin at the other extreme, expecting nothing,
and am always full of thanks for moderate goods.

Ralph Waldo Emerson

Enjoy the little things, for one day you may look back
and realize they were the big things.

Robert Brault

The little things? The little moments? They aren't little.

Jon Kabat-Zinn

Don't be afraid to give your best to
what seemingly are small jobs.
Every time you conquer one it makes you that much stronger.
If you do the little jobs well, the big ones will tend
to take care of themselves.

Dale Carnegie

Despise not small things....
A spark is a very little thing, yet it may kindle the world.

Martin Farquhar Tupper

The gifts we treasure most over the years
are often small and simple.
In easy times and in tough times, what seems to matter most
is the way we show those nearest us that we've been listening
to their needs, to their joys, and to their challenges.

Fred Rogers

All the wonderful things in life are so simple that one is
not aware of their wonder until they are beyond touch.

Frances Gunther

The simple life is one in which there is always time to remember the divine purpose behind each of our tasks, time to listen for a possible divine amendment to the day's schedule, and time to be thankful for the divine presence at each moment of the day.

Lloyd Lee Wilson

The ordinary arts we practice every day at home are of more importance to the soul than their simplicity might suggest.

Thomas Moore

A morning-glory at my window satisfies me more than the metaphysics of books.

Walt Whitman

It isn't the great big pleasures that count the most; it's making a great deal out of the little ones.

Jean Webster

To poke a wood fire is more solid enjoyment than almost anything else in the world.

Charles Dudley Warner

If people concentrated on the really important things in life,
there'd be a shortage of fishing poles.

Doug Larson

The next time you buy a microwaveable "dinner for two,"
think about the hour of free time you just gained.
Then spend that hour on something really important to you.

Odette Pollar

It is not what we take up, but what we
give up, that makes us rich.

Henry Ward Beecher

The art of being wise is the art of knowing what to overlook.

William James

The most important thing is to have a code of life,
to know how to live.

Hans Selye

We all have 100 percent to deal with in our lives:
10 percent is important,
90 percent is unimportant.
The secret to a happy, productive life
is to deal with the 10 percent and let the 90 percent slip.

Salli Rasberry and Padi Selwyn

Throw away your televisions. Practice critical thinking. Communicate with your family. Have social intercourse with your children. Play with them. Sing with them around the piano. Dance with them. Be foolish with them. Go out into the garden and have time to yourself.

Helen Caldicott

What lies behind us and what lies before us
are tiny matters compared to what lies within us.

Oliver Wendell Holmes

Remember, what you possess in the world will be found at the day of your death to belong to someone else, but what you are will be yours forever.

Henry van Dyke

Though we travel the world over to find the beautiful,
we must carry it with us or we find it not.

Ralph Waldo Emerson

I like living. I have sometimes been wildly, despairingly, acutely
miserable, racked with sorrow, but
through it all I still know quite
certainly that just to be alive is a grand thing.

Agatha Christie

How easily we get trapped in that which
is not essential—in looking
good, winning at competition, gathering
power and wealth—when
simply being alive is the gift beyond measure.

Parker J. Palmer

Forgive and Forget

One of the most beneficial things you can do to enhance your health and simplify your life is to let go of any grudges you may have toward someone else. Why? Because scientific research has found that not forgiving others can negatively impact both your mental and physical health.

In addition, it is a waste of time. The other person may not even know that you are carrying that bitterness. As actor Malachy McCourt reminds us in this section, "Resentment is like taking poison and waiting for the other person to die."

When you dwell in hatred and unforgiveness, you are triggering harmful emotions in your body. Even something that happened years ago can cause those resentments to rise up and take hold of your life again.

You may think that carrying a grudge gives you control over the situation, but, in reality, the situation is controlling you. Wouldn't you rather use that time more productively in more positive pursuits?

If you are having trouble forgiving someone, ask yourself, "Does holding onto my anger and resentment serve me?" Chances are it doesn't.

So, give yourself a gift. Find a quotation, or two, in this section that will lead you in the direction of forgiveness.

And though the following quotation by Mother Teresa is not elsewhere in this book, you might want to use it as a mantra as you go through your day:

"People are often unreasonable, illogical, and self-centered:
Forgive them anyway."

"I can forgive, but I cannot forget" is only another way of saying,
"I will not forgive."

Henry Ward Beecher

Life is an exercise in forgiveness.

Norman Cousins

To err is human, to forgive, divine.

Alexander Pope

Learn to forgive yourself and to forgive others.
Ask for forgiveness from others.
Forgiveness can soften the heart,
drain the bitterness, and dissolve your guilt.

Morrie Schwartz

He who cannot forgive others destroys the bridge
over which he himself must pass.

George Herbert

Forgive and you will be forgiven.

Luke 6:37

The creativity and positive energy you put forth come back
to you many times over. So do the hurt and destruction.
Which would you rather get back?

Ralph Marston

To forgive is the highest, most beautiful form of love.
In return, you will receive untold peace and happiness.

Robert Muller

Those who are at war with others
are not at peace with themselves.

William Hazlitt

Knowing life is short, how can we quarrel?

Buddha

If you want to get along, go along.

Sam Rayburn

To be wronged is nothing unless
you continue to remember it.

Confucius

If there's one pitch you keep swinging at and keep missing,
stop swinging at it.

Yogi Berra

Leave old baggage behind;
the less you carry, the farther you go.

Anonymous

May I forget what ought to be forgotten; and recall, unfailing,
all that ought to be recalled, each kindly thing,
forgetting what might sting.

Mary Carolyn Davies

Keeping score of old scores and scars, getting even
and one-upping always make you less than you are.

Malcolm Forbes

You never get ahead of anyone
as long as you try to get even with him.

Lou Holtz

Reject your sense of injury
and the injury itself disappears.

Marcus Aurelius

I can have peace of mind
only when I forgive rather than judge.

Gerald Jampolsky

Always forgive your enemies;
nothing annoys them so much.

Oscar Wilde

Resentment is like taking poison
and waiting for the other person to die.

Malachy McCourt

Forgiveness is a funny thing.
It warms the heart and cools the sting.

William A. Ward

Forgiveness is the answer to the child's dream of a miracle
by which what is broken is made whole again,
what is soiled is again made clean.

Catherine Ponder

In the end, forgiveness simply means
never putting another person out of our heart.

Jack Kornfield

Forgiveness is the key to action and freedom.

Hannah Arendt

If you want to see the brave, look for those who can forgive.

Bhagavad Gita

The weak can never forgive.
Forgiveness is the attribute of the strong.

Mahatma Gandhi

I believe with all my heart that civilization
has produced nothing
finer than a man or woman who thinks
and practices true tolerance.

Frank Knox

Forgiveness means letting go of the past.

Gerald Jampolsky

When you forgive, you in no way change the past—
but you sure do change the future.

Bernard Meltzer

Never do anything when you are in a temper,
for you will do everything wrong.

Baltasar Gracián

The elephant is never won with anger.

Earl of Rochester

Anyone can become angry—that is
easy. But to be angry with the
right person, to the right degree, at the
right time, for the right purpose,
and in the right way—that is not easy.

Aristotle

The more anger toward the past you carry in your heart,
the less capable you are of loving in the present.

Barbara De Angelis

For every minute you are angry,
you lose sixty seconds of happiness.

Ralph Waldo Emerson

Write injuries in dust, benefits in marble.

Benjamin Franklin

Anger is a lot like a piece of shredded wheat caught
under your dentures. If you leave it there, you'll
get a blister and you gotta eat Jell-O all week.
If you get rid of it, the sore heals and you feel better.

Sophia Petrillo, The Golden Girls

Ask yourself this question:
"Will this matter a year from now?"

Richard Carlson

Go with the Flow

An age-old story, sometimes attributed to the Chinese philosopher Lao-Tzu and other times to Confucius, tells of an old man who accidentally fell into the river rapids leading to a high and dangerous waterfall. Onlookers feared for his life. Miraculously, he came out alive and unharmed downstream at the bottom of the falls. People asked him how he managed to survive.

"I accommodated myself to the water. I allowed myself to be shaped by it. Plunging into the swirl, I came out with the swirl. This is how I survived."

There is an important lesson here for all of us today. Instead of resisting the unexpected, sometimes painful things life hands us, we would be much wiser to accept them. Resisting those things only opens the door to added pain. When we don't let go and accept the way things are, when we continually struggle to change them, we suffer. The way to avoid suffering, then, is to go with the flow of life.

Letting go and going with the flow is easier said than done, of course, but it is possible. The thoughts in this section can help you do that. My favorite is by the founder of "est," Werner Erhard, who playfully said, "It's much easier to ride the horse in the direction he's going."

Better bend than break.

H. G. Bohn

The bamboo that bends is stronger than the oak that resists.

Japanese proverb

If you can't fight and you can't flee, flow.

Robert S. Eliot

It's much easier to ride the horse in the direction he's going.

Werner Erhard

You have freedom when you're easy in your harness.

Robert Frost

Develop a mind that is vast like the water, where experiences both pleasant and unpleasant can appear and disappear without conflict, struggle, or harm. Rest in a mind like vast water.

Buddha

I began to have an idea for my life, not as the slow shaping of
achievement to fit my preconceived purposes,
but as the gradual
discovery and growth of a purpose which I did not know.

Joanna Field

Sometimes you've got to let everything go—purge yourself.
If you are unhappy with anything...
whatever is bringing you down,
get rid of it. Because you'll find that when you're free,
your true creativity, your true self comes out.

Tina Turner

Somehow, when we no longer feel in control,
we become available to deeper aliveness.

Richard Moss

Not trying to go faster or slower,
be still, and let go.
Just let things be
for it is exactly as it should be.

Sosan

Things turn out best for the people who make the best
of the way things turn out.

John Wooden

Live with less grasping and
more appreciation and caring.

Jack Kornfield

Eventually I lost interest in trying to control my life,
to make things happen in a way that I
thought I wanted them to be.
I began to practice surrounding to the universe
and finding out what "it" wanted me to do.

Shakti Gawain

As your faith is strengthened, you will find that there
is no longer the need to have a sense of control, that
things will flow as they will, and that you will flow
with them, to your great delight and benefit.

Emmanuel Teney

There is no good in arguing with the
inevitable. The only argument
available with an east wind is to put on your overcoat.

James Russell Lowell

When you're in a state of nonacceptance, it's difficult to learn.
A clenched fist cannot receive a gift, and a clenched psyche—
grasped tightly against the reality of
what must not be accepted—
cannot easily receive a lesson.

John-Roger and Peter McWilliams

You can't fit a square peg into a round hole....
Think how simple your life would be if
you eliminated the difficult
things—the things that probably weren't
meant to be anyway—and
concentrated instead on doing what was easy.

Elaine St. James

The worst thing you can do is to try to cling to something
that's gone, or to recreate it.

Johnette Napolitano

The bird of paradise alights
only upon the hand that does not grasp.

John Berry

Grow Down

When I was a young child, one of my favorite toys was a red metal moving truck, about two-and-a-half feet long. Nearly every day I would sit on top of it and "drive" it down the long hallway of our apartment. Once I got to the other end, I'd open the rear doors and unload what was in it. Then I would reload the truck with other toys and ride back to the other end of the foyer.

I would occupy myself for hours by doing this over and over again. I was the moving man delivering important goods across the country. My imagination was the key for me and my moving truck riding the great highway in the hall.

There were no video games on the Internet or smartphones then. Nor did my family own a television set. It was a simpler time with less available choices, but an unlimited abundance of choices within my imagination.

Because many great achievements start in someone's mind, we not only need to encourage more playful imagination in children, but also ask adults to grow down and be more childlike in order to nurture their imaginations too.

As author Ursula K. Le Guin tells us in this section, "As great scientists have said and as all children know, it is above all by the imagination that we achieve perception, and compassion, and hope."

Return to the beginning; become a child again.

Lao-Tzu

Genius is the ability to regain childhood at will.

Anonymous

Youth would be an ideal state if it came a little later in life.

Herbert Henry Asquith

You can learn new things at any time in your life
if you're willing to be a beginner. If you actually learn to
like being a beginner, the whole world opens up to you.

Barbara Sher

The parents exist to teach the child,
but also they must learn what the child has to teach them,
and the child has a very great deal to teach them.

Arnold Bennett

The first problem for all of us, men and women,
is not to learn, but to unlearn.

Gloria Steinem

My music is best understood by children and animals.

Igor Stravinsky

There are children playing in the streets who could solve
some of my top problems in physics, because they have
modes of sensory perception that I lost long ago.

J. Robert Oppenheimer

Wisdom sends us back to our childhood.

Blaise Pascal

Seek the wisdom of the ages,
but look at the world through the eyes of a child.

Ron Wild

Look at everything as though you were seeing it
either for the first or last time.

Betty Smith

The voyage of discovery lies not in finding new landscapes,
but in having new eyes.

Marcel Proust

As great scientists have said and as all children know,
it is above all by the imagination that we achieve perception,
and compassion, and hope.

Ursula K. Le Guin

It is the childlike mind that finds the kingdom.

Charles Fillmore

If help and salvation are to come, they can only come from
the children, for the children are the makers of men.

Maria Montessori

If my heart can become pure and simple like that of a child,
I think there probably can be no greater happiness than this.

Kitaro Nishida

Is nothing in life ever straight and clear, the way children see it?

Rosie Thomas

Pretty much all the honest truth telling there is in the world
is done by children.

Oliver Wendell Holmes

In every real man a child is hidden that wants to play.

Friedrich Wilhelm Nietzsche

It is paradoxical that many educators
and parents still differentiate
between a time for learning and a time for play
without seeing the vital connection between them.

Leo Buscaglia

In reality, we are still children. We want to find a playmate
for our thoughts and feelings.

Wilhelm Stekel

Man is most nearly himself when he achieves the seriousness
of a child at play.

Heraclitus

We live in an ironic society where even play is turned into work,
but the highest existence is not work;
the highest level of existence is play.

Conrad Hyers

People do not quit playing because they grow old.
They grow old because they quit playing.

Oliver Wendell Holmes

Can you imagine experiencing the world as a great sandbox given for us to play in like we did as children? As we play, we can also open ourselves to the exploration of our edges, always creating new adventures of self-exploration as we let go of old outdated beliefs about ourselves.

Judith-Annette Milburn

It may well be that all games are silly.
But then—so are human beings.

Robert Lynd

If it seems a childish thing to do,
do it in remembrance that you were a child.

Frederick Buechner

Hang around doggies and kids: they know how to play.

Geoffrey Godbey

The child is in me still...and sometimes not so still.

Fred Rogers

If you listen carefully to children,
you will have plenty about which to laugh.

Steve Allen

Know you what it is to be a child? It is to be something very
different from the man of today. It is
to have a spirit yet steaming
from the water of baptism; it is to believe in love, to believe in
loveliness, to believe in belief; it is to
be so little that the elves can
reach to whisper in your ear; it is to
turn pumpkins into coaches,
and mice into horses, lowness into loftiness, and nothing into
everything, for each child has its fairy godmother in its soul.

Francis Thompson

Every child comes with the message
that God is not yet tired of the man.

Rabindranath Tagore

The secret of genius is
to carry the spirit of the child into old age.

Thomas Huxley

Great is the man who has not lost his childlike heart.

Mencius

By learning to act more like a child,
human beings can revolutionize
their lives and become for the first time, perhaps, the kinds of
creatures their heritage has prepared them to be—
youthful all the days of their lives.

Ashley Montagu

Have Less

Whenever my birthday rolls around, friends and family often ask what they can get me to celebrate the occasion. I tell them that I don't want more stuff. I have more than enough stuff. I want an experience, something that will live forever in my memory. From a lifetime of collecting, I know that the more things I have, the more time I need to devote to organizing them, cleaning them, or making sure I don't break them.

In fact, I'm going through something like that right now. Several years ago, I sold a second home I had in a rural area outside of San Francisco. When I first moved there, I brought all my vinyl records with me. When the house sold, I took all of them back to the city and stored them in the guest room. With the advent of CDs and downloadable music from the Internet, I no longer listened to records. Still, I hung on to them.

For over two-and-a-half years, they sat in the guest room, sometimes needing to be moved when a houseguest arrived. I'd often look at the records and think I should sell them. But I never acted upon it. Until now.

A relative will be arriving next week. This time, the records have to go. I've contacted a record shop who will be coming by to purchase them. I will miss some because of the fond memories I have of listening to the recordings. I also know that I can probably get any one of those songs on the Internet. I also know that in having less, I have—as one author in the following section tells us—opened up both a physical and metaphorical space in my life. For that I am most grateful.

The most important things in life aren't things.

Anonymous

If there is to be any peace, it will come
through being, not having.

Henry Miller

Most of the luxuries, and many of the so-called comforts of life,
are not only not indispensable, but positive hindrances
to the elevation of mankind.

Henry David Thoreau

Joy is not in things; it is in us.

Richard Wagner

Be not anxious about what you have, but about what you are.

Pope St. Gregory I

Superfluous wealth can buy superfluities only.
Money is not required to buy one necessity of the soul.

Henry David Thoreau

True abundance is not about gathering more things,
it's about touching the place in us that is connected to the
divine source of abundance, so that we know what we
need in the moment will be provided.

Mary Manin Morrissey

Own only what you can always carry with you; know languages,
know countries, know people. Let your
memory be your travel bag.

Alexander Solzhenitsyn

Be content with what you have, rejoice in the way things are.
When you realize there is nothing lacking,
the whole world belongs to you.

Lao-Tzu

Use it up, wear it out, make it do, or do without.

New England proverb

We never buy more than we need.
We never need more than we use.
We never use more than
it takes to get by
'til we learn to need less.

Chinese proverb

Have fewer things and see each of them better.

Odette Pollar

Know what is enough. If you think that having more
is what is going to produce happiness
or contentment or any positive attribute,
will you ever get there?

Joe Dominguez

You have succeeded in life when all you really want
is only what you really need.

Vernon Howard

Make peace with the awareness that you
can't have everything you want.
It's more important for you to get everything you need.
Contentment comes when our essential needs are met.

Sarah Ban Breathnach

If you always want "more" you will never have "enough."

Ken Keyes, Jr. and Bruce Burkan

There must be more to life than having everything.

Maurice Sendak

You can't have it all—where would you put it?

Steven Wright

You can have anything you want.
You just can't have everything you want.

John-Roger and Peter McWilliams

You can never get enough of what you don't need
to make you happy.

Eric Hoffer

If men could regard the events of their own lives
with more open minds, they would frequently discover
that they did not really desire the things
they failed to obtain.

Emile Herzog

The cost of a thing
is the amount of what I call life
which is required to be exchanged for it.

Henry David Thoreau

My riches consist not in the extent of my possessions,
but in the fewness of my wants.

J. Brotherton

We don't need to increase our goods nearly as much
as we need to scale down our wants.
Not wanting something is as good as possessing it.

Donald Horban

When you can't have what you want,
it's time to start wanting what you have.

Kathleen A. Sutton

He who is attached to things will suffer much.

Lao-Tzu

Possessions are usually diminished by possession.

Friedrich Wilhelm Nietzsche

Simplicity is not so much about what we own,
but about what owns us.

Christin Hadley Snyder

All things that a man owns hold him
far more than he holds them.

Sigrid Undset

It is preoccupation with possessions, more than anything else,
that prevents us from living freely and nobly.

Bertrand Russell

He who buys what he does not need steals from himself.

Anonymous

Possession of material riches without inner peace
is like dying of thirst while bathing in the river.

Paramahansa Yogananda

Those who want the fewest things are nearest to the gods.

Socrates

Happiness resides not in possessions and not in gold,
the feeling of happiness dwells in the soul.

Democritus

As for things, how they do accumulate,
how often I wish to exclaim,
"Oh, don't give me that!"

Susan Hale

The more we reduce the size of our world,
the more we shall be its master.

Jacinto Benavente

Through the years I have found it wonderful to acquire,
but it is also wonderful to divest. It's rather like exhaling.

Helen Hayes

Reduce the complexity of life by eliminating the needless
wants of life, and the labors of life reduce themselves.

Edwin Way Teale

That man is the richest
whose pleasures are the cheapest.

Henry David Thoreau

To know you have enough is to be rich.

Lao-Tzu

Frugality is one of the most beautiful and joyful words
in the English language, and yet one that we are culturally
cut off from understanding and enjoying.
The consumption society
has made us feel that happiness lies in having things and has
failed to teach us the happiness of not having things.

Elise Boulding

One day I had the sudden realization: if I stopped buying things
right this moment, there is no way I
could ever use all I have now.

Don Aslett

The richest person is the one who is
contented with what he has.

Robert C. Savage

Even though you have ten thousand fields,
you can eat no more than one measure of rice a day.
Even though your dwelling contains a hundred rooms,
you can use but eight feet of space a night.

Chinese proverb

Riches do not consist in the possession of treasures,
but in the use made of them.

Napoleon Bonaparte

If you want a golden rule that will fit everybody, this is it:
have nothing in your house that you do not know
to be useful or believe to be beautiful.

William Morris

Too many people spend money they
haven't earned, to buy things
they don't want, to impress people they don't like.

Will Rogers

Normal is getting dressed in clothes
that you buy for work, driving
through traffic in a car that you are still paying for, in order to
get to the job that you need so you can pay for the clothes,
car, and the house that you leave empty all day
in order to afford to live in it.

Ellen Goodman

Let the potent power of simplicity begin to work in your life.
When in doubt, live without.

Sarah Ban Breathnach

Notice to Guests: if there is anything you need and don't see,
please let us know; we will show you how to do without it.

Mary McWilliams Fadden

To be without some of the things you want
is an indispensable part of happiness.

Bertrand Russell

Simplicity, simplicity, simplicity! I say let your affairs be as one,
two, three and not a hundred or a thousand.... We are happy
in proportion to the things we can do without.

Henry David Thoreau

Let your boat of life be light,
packed with only what you need.

Jerome K. Jerome

Keep It Simple

I have heard that the actor Mandy Patinkin only owns black clothing. I also have a friend whose clothes are all black. And I had another friend who only ate oatmeal for breakfast, every day, every week, every month.

It is certainly a way to simplify some things in your life. If you only had black garments, you'd never have to decide if any one piece of clothing matched another or if they clashed. At breakfast, you would never have to waste time deciding what to eat.

While these might be good ideas to simplify certain aspects of your life, they would not be my choice. Yes, I wear black sometimes, but I like color; in fact, I have several racks of bright, colorful ties. I also eat oatmeal about once a week, but vary that with breakfasts of eggs, pancakes, or cold cereal.

The essence of this book is all about uncomplicating your life. There are hundreds of ways to do that. Simplifying your clothes selection or breakfast choices is only one way. You need to decide what yours will be. I hope the thoughts in this book will inspire you and help you move in that direction.

'Tis a gift to be simple,
'tis a gift to be free.

Shaker hymn

I have come to understand that making life simpler does
for our minds what getting in shape does for our bodies.

Robert Lawrence Smith

In order to see one's own direction,
one must simplify the mechanics of ordinary everyday life.

Plato

You know it's time to simplify your life when
you've got a ringing phone in one hand,
a hot double cappuccino mocha in the other,
and you need to make a left-hand turn.

Elaine St. James

Achieving simplicity in your life starts with the simple notion
that you are in control. You steer the rudder, flip the switch,
pull the lever, call the shots, and have the power within you
to take steps to make your life simpler.

Jeff Davidson

Voluntary simplicity means going fewer places in one day
rather than more, seeing less so I can see more, doing less
so I can do more, acquiring less so I can have more.

Jon Kabat-Zinn

You can't force simplicity, but you can invite it in by
finding as much richness as possible in the few things at hand.
Simplicity doesn't mean meagerness but rather a certain kind
of richness, the fullness that appears when we stop
stuffing the world with things.

Thomas Moore

If I were asked to define Quaker simplicity in a nutshell,
I would say that it has little to do with
how many things you own
and everything to do with not letting your possessions own you.

Robert Lawrence Smith

Simplicity was my protection when I first was born...

Thomas Traherne

The ability to simplify means to eliminate the unnecessary
so that the necessary may speak.

Hans Hofmann

In the end, what affects your life most deeply
are things too simple to talk about.

Nell Blaine

Simplicity involves unburdening your
life and living more lightly
with fewer distractions that interfere with a high quality life,
as defined uniquely by each individual.
You will find people living simply in large cities,
rural areas, and everything in between.

Linda Breen Pierce

Life comes together when we seek of
the sublime in the ordinary.
Today, make discovering those joyful simplicities that bring
you personal comfort and a sense of well-being
one of your highest priorities.

Sarah Ban Breathnach

Your wishes were too simple: or too complex.

Frank Bidart

To live content with small means...this is my symphony.

William Henry Channing

When hungry, eat your rice; when tired, close your eyes.
Fools may laugh at me, but wise men will know what I mean.

Linji Yixuan

To own a bit of ground, to scratch it
with a hoe, to plant seeds and
watch their renewal of life—this is the commonest delight of the
race, the most satisfactory things a man can do.

Charles Dudley Warner

It is difficult to think anything but pleasant thoughts
while eating a home-grown tomato.

Lewis Grizzard

You know it's time to simplify your life when you
just published your third book on how to get organized,
and you can't find it.

Elaine St. James

Simplicity doesn't mean to live in misery and poverty.
You have what you need, and you don't want to have
what you don't need.

Charan Singh

Simplicity is the most difficult thing to secure in this
world; it is the last limit of experience
and the last effort of genius.

George Sand

Simplicity is the nature of great souls.

Papa Ramadas

Make everything as simple as possible, but not simpler.

Albert Einstein

Any intelligent fool can make things bigger, more complex, and
more violent. It takes a touch of genius—and a lot of courage—
to move in the opposite direction.

E. F. Schumacher

A man must be able to cut a knot, for
everything cannot be untied;
he must know how to disengage what
is essential from the detail in
which it is enwrapped, for everything
cannot be equally considered;
in a word, he must be able to simplify his duties,
his business and his life.

Henri Frédéric Amiel

True simplicity is not the rejection of beauty
in our surroundings, but the refusal to allow concern
for things to clutter our minds.

Edgar B. Castle

Out of clutter, find simplicity.

Albert Einstein

Simplicity is the whole secret of well-being.

Peter Matthiessen

In walking, just walk. In sitting, just sit. Above all, don't wobble.

Yunmen

A little simplification would be the first step
toward rational living, I think.

Eleanor Roosevelt

I have a simple philosophy. Fill what's empty.
Empty what's full. Scratch where it itches.

Alice Roosevelt Longworth

I believe that a simple and unassuming manner of life
is best for everyone, best for the body and the mind.

Albert Einstein

Simplicity, clarity, singleness: these are the attributes
that give our lives power and vividness and joy...

Richard Holloway

Simplicity is the essence of happiness.

Cedric Bledsoe

Purity and simplicity are the two wings with which man soars
above the earth and all temporary nature.

Thomas à Kempis

In character, in manners, in style, in all things,
the supreme excellence is simplicity.

Henry Wadsworth Longfellow

Life is not complex. We are complex. Life is simple,
and the simple thing is the right thing.

Oscar Wilde

I have learned by some experience, by many examples,
and by the writings of countless others before me,
also occupied in the search, that certain environments,
certain modes of life, certain rules of conduct are more
conducive to inner and outer harmony than others.
There are, in fact, certain roads that one may follow.
Simplification of life is one of them.

Anne Morrow Lindbergh

Life is really simple, but we insist on making it complicated.

Confucius

Manifest plainness,
embrace simplicity,
reduce selfishness,
have few desires.

Lao-Tzu

The right thing to do never requires any subterfuge,
it is always simple and direct.

Calvin Coolidge

I searched through rebellion, drugs, diets, mysticism,
religions, intellectualism and much more,
only to begin to find...that truth is
basically simple—and feels good, clean, and right.

Chick Corea

All the great things are simple, and many can be expressed in a single word: freedom, justice, honor, duty, mercy, hope.

Sir Winston Churchill

Simplicity of life, even the barest, is not a misery,
but the very foundation of refinement.

William Morris

Simplicity is the ultimate sophistication.

Leonardo da Vinci

In cooking, as in all the arts, simplicity is the sign of perfection.

Curnonsky

There is no greatness where there is not simplicity.

Leo Tolstoy

The aspects of things that are most important to us
are hidden because of their simplicity and familiarity.

Ludwig Wittgenstein

I thank you, my God, for having in a
thousand different ways led my
eyes to discover the immense simplicity of things.

Pierre Teilhard de Chardin

Rose is a rose is a rose is a rose.

Gertrude Stein

You see, God always takes the simplest way.

Albert Einstein

Life is beautiful in its simplicity.

Thomas Matthiessen

Live simply so others may simply live.

Sister Joan Puls

Savor Silence

Years ago, whenever I visited New York City, I would stay with one of my favorite cousins. I loved being with her, but there was one thing that really annoyed me. She would constantly have the television blaring, even though she wasn't even watching it most of the time.

The experience made me realize how much I treasure silence. I need it to calm me down. I need it to balance a noisy world. I need it when I'm writing. In fact, when I'm at my computer, I often use earplugs so that I feel totally alone with my thoughts and my words.

Perhaps I'm old-fashioned for craving silence. After all, these days, the constant addiction to noise seems to be the norm. Most Millennials, for example, seem to be permanently engulfed in some sort of sound; they are forever hooked up to earbuds or work on their computers in loud Internet cafés.

If you are constantly surrounded by the clatter of sound, I suggest you find a quiet place to experience some silence. And while you may feel that silence produces nothing and that you are wasting your time, you are wrong. Silence has the potential to enrich everything in your life. As the author Anne Morrow Lindberg reminds us in this section, "A note of music gains significance from the silence on either side."

Speech is silver; silence is golden.

Swiss proverb

True silence is the rest of the mind, and
is to the spirit what sleep is
to the body, nourishment and refreshment.

William Penn

In...silence we find a new energy and a real unity. God's energy becomes ours, allowing us to perform things well.

Mother Teresa

The first virtue is to restrain the tongue;
he approaches nearest to the gods who knows how to be silent....

Cato the Younger

Silence is the true friend that never betrays.

Confucius

The Great Way is empty—
like a vast sky.
Silence the busy mind
and know this perfection.

Sosan

The deepest feeling always shows itself in silence.

Marianne Moore

Occasionally in life there are those moments of unutterable
fulfillment which cannot be completely
explained by those symbols
called words. Their meanings can only be articulated
by the inaudible language of the heart.

Martin Luther King, Jr.

A loving silence often has far more power to heal and
to connect than the most well-intentioned words.

Rachel Naomi Remen

There is something greater and purer
than what the mouth utters.
Silence illuminates our souls, whispers to our hearts,
and brings them together.

Kahlil Gibran

In the attitude of silence the soul finds the path
in a clearer light, and what is elusive and deceptive
resolves itself into crystal clearness.

Mahatma Gandhi

God is the friend of silence. See how nature—trees, flowers,
grass—grows in silence; see the stars, the moon and the sun,
how they move in silence...we need silence
to be able to touch souls.

Mother Teresa

Sitting quietly, doing nothing, spring comes,
and the grass grows by itself.

Zen saying

We in the "developed" world seem to have many auditory
strategies that insulate us from the
presence of silence, simplicity,
and solitude. When I return to Western
culture after time in desert,
mountain, or forest, I discover how we have filled our world
with a multiplicity of noises, a symphony of forgetfulness
that keeps our own thoughts and realizations,
feelings and intuitions out of audible range.

Joan Halifax

Soon silence will have passed into legend. Man has turned
his back on silence. Day after day, he invents machines
and devices that increase noise and distract humanity
from the essence of life, contemplation, meditation.

Jean Arp

Why are we embarrassed by silence?
What comfort do we find in all the noise?

Mitch Albom

An inability to stay quiet...
is one of the most conspicuous failings of mankind.

Walter Bagehot

The more we elaborate our means of communication,
the less we communicate.

J. B. Priestly

Perhaps it would be a good idea, fantastic as it sounds, to muffle
every telephone, stop every motor and
halt all activity for an hour
some day to give people a chance to
ponder for a few minutes on
what it is all about, why they are living
and what they really want.

James Truslow Adams

No one has a finer command of language
than the person who keeps his mouth shut.

Sam Rayburn

A man is known by the silence he keeps.

Oliver Herford

In Maine we have a saying that there's no point in speaking unless you can improve on silence.

Edmund Muskie

It's amazing how much you hear
when no one is saying anything.

Elaine St. James

There are very few people who don't become more interesting when they stop talking.

Mary Lowry

I have never been hurt by anything I didn't say.

Calvin Coolidge

You don't always have to have something to say.

Sammy Davis, Jr.

When you have nothing to say, say nothing.

Charles Caleb Colton

The value of the average conversation
could be enormously improved by the constant use
of four simple words: "I do not know."

André Maurois

It has been said: lots of things are opened by mistake,
but none so often as the mouth.

Gladys Case

Stop talking and listen to what you really know.

Robert Lawrence Smith

Only in the oasis of silence can we drink deeply
from the inner cup of wisdom.

Sue Patton Thoele

A spiritual retreat is medicine for soul starvation. Through silence, solitary practice, and simple living, we begin to fill the empty reservoir. This lifts the veils, dissolves the masks, and creates space within for the feelings of forgiveness, compassion, and loving kindness that are so often blocked.

David A. Cooper

Silence fertilizes the deep place where personality grows.
A life with a peaceful center can weather all storms.

Norman Vincent Peale

One's action ought to come out of an achieved stillness,
not to be a mere rushing on.

D. H. Lawrence

Well-timed silence is the most commanding expression.

Mark Helprin

The silence is as important as the noise. What gets left out
is as important as what gets included.

Sara Lawrence-Lightfoot

A note of music gains significance
from the silence on either side.

Anne Morrow Lindbergh

The notes I handle no better than any pianist. But the pauses
between the notes—ah, that is where the art resides!

Artur Schnabel

Only in quiet waters do things mirror themselves undistorted.
Only in a quiet mind is adequate perception of the world.

Hans Margolius

Men cannot see their reflection in running water,
but only in still water.

Chuang Tzu

I have often thought it would be a blessing if each human being
were stricken blind and deaf for a few
days during his early adult life.
Darkness would make him more appreciative of sight;
silence would teach him the joys of sound.

Helen Keller

Learn to get in touch with silence within yourself and know
that everything in this life has a purpose. There are no mistakes,
no coincidences; all events are blessings
given to us to learn from.
There is no need to go to India or anywhere else to find peace.
You will find that deep place of silence right in your room,
your garden, or even your bathtub.

Elisabeth Kübler-Ross

To experience reality,
stop using words;
for the more you talk about things,
the farther away from the truth you stray.

Sosan

Seek Solitude

Several years ago, I owned a house in a rural part of Northern California. I used to joke that it had a partial ocean view because if I walked a short way down the dirt road, I could see a sliver of the ocean glistening between the distant hills.

Although the house didn't really have an ocean view, nor one of surrounding mountains, it did have a view that pleased my soul. It had a small meadow with a line of fruit trees that provided the backdrop for a level grassy area. It is where I planted a vegetable garden, where the gladiolas bloomed along the pathway and where the grapes, which mostly fed the birds, grew.

There wasn't much to look at in the meadow, but I could sit at the kitchen table for long periods of time, silently viewing the wonder of nature. Having grown up in the city all of my life, I felt like I was a voyeur watching a world that both nourished and calmed me.

Sitting in solitude, I saw a leaf slowly float to the ground as the wind gently shook the tree. I noticed that the bright blue morning glories had opened now that the sun was on them. I delighted in seeing a rare yellow canary bird pick at some berries. And so much more.

For a view with no sweeping panorama or expanse of rolling ocean waves, it was glorious. And all because I sat silently for a while and let the life of the meadow unfold before me.

Our language has wisely sensed the two sides of being alone.
It has created the word "loneliness" to express the pain of being alone. And it has created the word "solitude" to express the glory of being alone.

Paul Tillich

Loneliness is the poverty of self; solitude is the richness of self.

May Sarton

Nothing will change the fact that I cannot produce the least thing without absolute solitude.

Johann Wolfgang von Goethe

It would do the world good if every man
in it would compel himself
occasionally to be absolutely alone.
Most of the world's progress
has come out of such loneliness.

Bruce Barton

We need society, and we need solitude also, as we need summer and winter, day and night, exercise and rest.

Philip Gilbert Hamerton

We need quiet time to examine our lives openly and
honestly...spending quiet time alone gives your mind
an opportunity to renew itself and create order.

Susan L. Taylor

Only when one is connected to one's
own core is one connected to
others. And, for me, the core, the inner spring,
can best be refound through solitude.

Anne Morrow Lindbergh

What a lovely surprise to finally discover
how unlonely being alone can be.

Ellen Burstyn

It isn't only famous movie stars who want to be alone.
Whenever I hear someone speak of
privacy, I find myself thinking
once again how real and deep the need for such times is for all
human beings...at all ages.

Fred Rogers

The best thinking has been done in solitude.
The worst has been done in turmoil.

Thomas Edison

Conversation enriches the understanding,
but solitude is the school of genius.

Edward Gibbon

Great decisions in the realms of thought and
momentous discoveries and solutions of problems
are only possible to an individual working in solitude.

Sigmund Freud

There are voices which we hear in
solitude, but they grow faint and
inaudible as we enter into the world.

Ralph Waldo Emerson

A master needs quiet. Calm and quiet are his most imperative
needs. Isolation and complete loneliness
are my only consolation,
and my salvation.

Richard Wagner

If the mind loves solitude, it has thereby acquired a loftier
character, and it becomes nobler when the taste is indulged in.

Wilhelm von Humboldt

I never found the companion
that was so companionable as solitude.

Henry David Thoreau

The great man is he who, in the midst of the world,
keeps with perfect sweetness the independence of solitude.

Ralph Waldo Emerson

Never be afraid to sit awhile and think.

Lorraine Hansberry

Meditation is the soul's perspective glass.

Owen Feltham

Contemplation is the highest form of activity.

Aristotle

Sit in reverie, and watch the changing color of the waves
that break upon the idle seashore of the mind.

Henry Wadsworth Longfellow

Happiness is a butterfly which, when pursued,
is always beyond our grasp, but which, if you will
sit down quietly, may alight upon you.

Nathaniel Hawthorne

You do not need to leave your room. Remain sitting
at your table and listen. Do not even listen, simply wait.
Do not even wait, be quite still and solitary. The world will
freely offer itself to you to be unmasked, it has no choice,
it will roll in ecstasy at your feet.

Franz Kafka

Ah! There's nothing like staying home for real comfort.

Jane Austen

I sat in my sunny doorway from sunrise
till noon, rapt in a reverie
amidst the pines and hickories and
sumacs, in undisturbed solitude
and stillness, while the birds sing around or flitted noiseless
through the house.... I grew in those
seasons like corn in the night.

Henry David Thoreau

Solitude is a silent storm that breaks down
all our dead branches; yet it sends our living roots
deeper into the living heart of the living earth.

Kahlil Gibran

Solitude is the place of purification.

Martin Buber

Like water which can clearly mirror the sky and the trees only
so long as its surface is undisturbed,
the mind can only reflect the
true image of the Self when it is tranquil and wholly relaxed.

Indra Devi

In the solitude of your mind are the
answers to all your questions
about life. You must take the time to ask and listen.

Bawa Muhaiyaddeen

Unlike achieving things worth having, to achieve things
worth being usually requires long periods of solitude.

Meyer Friedman and Ray Rosenman

There is one art of which man should be master,
the art of reflection.

Samuel Taylor Coleridge

I love people. I love my family, my children...but inside myself
is a place where I live all alone and that's where you renew
your springs that never dry up.

Pearl S. Buck

It is in deep solitude that I find the gentleness
with which I can truly love my brothers.

Thomas Merton

Get away from the crowd when you can.
Keep yourself to yourself,
if only for a few hours daily.

Arthur Brisbane

You must have a room, or a certain hour a day or so,
where you do not know what was in the newspapers...
a place where you can simply experience and bring forth
what you are and what you might be.

Joseph Campbell

[Going to a retreat] has something to do
with an aspect within each
one of us...unknown to science...that longs to be at peace.

David A. Cooper

In solitude we give passionate attention to our lives,
to our memories, to the details around us.

Virginia Woolf

When we cannot bear to be alone, it means we do not
properly value the only companion we will have
from birth to death—ourselves.

Eda LeShan

When I dance, I dance, when I sleep, I sleep; yes,
and when I walk alone in a beautiful orchard, if my thoughts
drift to far-off matters for some part of the time, for some
other part I lead them back again to the walk, the orchard,
to the sweetness of this solitude, to myself.

Michel de Montaigne

I will tell you what I have learned myself.
For me a long, five- or six-mile
walk helps. And one must go alone and every day.

Brenda Ueland

All walking is discovery.
On foot we take the time to see things whole.

Hal Borland

The best remedy for those who are afraid, lonely, or unhappy is to go outside, somewhere where they can be quiet, alone with the heavens, nature, and God. Because only then does one feel that all is as it should be and that God wishes to see people happy, amidst the simple beauty of nature.

Anne Frank

One can be instructed in society,
one is inspired only in solitude.

Johann Wolfgang von Goethe

Shun Perfection

Unity San Francisco is a spiritual community to which I belong. Every week during the Sunday service, we bring the children of the congregation on stage and bless them with the following affirmation: "You are God's perfect child. We love you just the way you are."

Even though we are aiming that toward all the children in the room, we also extend that affirmation to every adult and their inner child.

What we are saying is that every single one of us is loveable just the way we are, even with our flaws and blemishes. When we truly know that, we can stop disliking aspects of ourselves and embrace our imperfections. In fact, it is often because of these flaws that we are special and unique.

A number of entertainers know this. They have physical flaws and have achieved stardom in spite of their imperfections. One of them is supermodel and actress Cindy Crawford. She has a mole above her lip—not the greatest asset for someone whose career involves being picture perfect. Still, she says, "I often tell young women that my shortcoming became my trademark, and I encourage them to love everything about themselves—even the parts which are not perfect."

Hopefully the quotations in this section will help you realize that there is no need to chase perfection since everything in your life is already perfect when you choose to see it that way.

The game is supposed to be fun. If you have a bad day,
don't worry about it. You can't expect to get a hit every game.

Yogi Berra

You're only human, you're supposed to make mistakes.

Billy Joel

How much of our lives is frittered away—spoiled, spent,
or sullied—by our neurotic insistence on perfection?

Sarah Ban Breathnach

Perfectionism is the voice of the oppressor,
the enemy of the people.
It will keep you cramped and insane your whole life.

Anne Lamott

Perfection does not exist. To understand this
is the triumph of human intelligence;
to expect to possess it is the most dangerous kind of madness.

Alfred de Musset

Perfection is an elusive butterfly.
When we cease to demand perfection,
the business of being happy becomes that much easier.

Helen Keller

People throw away what they could have by
insisting on perfection, which they cannot have,
and looking for it where they will never find it.

Edith Schaeffer

Have no fear of perfection—you'll never reach it.

Salvador Dali

Striving for excellence motivates you;
striving for perfection is demoralizing.

Harriet Beryl Braiker

A man would do nothing if he waited
until he could do it so well
that no one could find fault.

John Henry Newman

Perfection consists not in doing extraordinary things,
but in doing ordinary things extraordinarily well.

Angelique Arnauld

Don't be afraid to admit that you are less than perfect.
It is this fragile thread that binds us to each other.

Brian Dyson

What, after all, is a halo? It's only one more thing to keep clean.

Christopher Fry

When everything has to be right, something isn't.

Stanislaw Lec

Life does not have to be perfect to be wonderful.

Annette Funicello

A good garden may have some weeds.

Thomas Fuller

Slow Down

I have noticed that when I'm rushing around, I get overly anxious. As a result, things often don't turn out well. I dash out of my house only to discover that I left behind something I needed. I'm in a hurry to get to an appointment, so I jump out of the car, leaving my keys locked inside. I rush around the kitchen to get ready for dinner guests and realize I forgot to add an ingredient to the cake baking in the oven.

When I slow down, on the other hand, I make better decisions with more clarity because I am calmer and more centered. Also, as author Alexandra Potter so eloquently describes in her book *The Two Lives of Miss Charlotte Merryweather*, one of the greatest benefits of slowing down is its ability to enhance and enrich our lives:

> And so taking the long way home through the market I slow my pace down. It doesn't come naturally. My legs are programmed to trot briskly and my arms to pump up and down like pistons, but I force myself to stroll past the stalls and pavement cafés. To enjoy just being somewhere, rather than rushing from somewhere, to somewhere. Inhaling deep lungfuls of air, instead of my usual shallow breaths. I take a moment to just stop and look around me. And smile to myself.
>
> For the first time in a long time, I can, quite literally, smell the coffee.

Stop, slow down, embrace a quotation or two from this section, and let their words help you, too, smell the coffee (or Earl Grey tea, if you prefer).

Go slowly, breathe and smile.

Thich Nhat Hanh

Life is not a race, but a journey to be
savored each step of the way.

Brian Dyson

In the name of God,
stop a moment, cease your work, look around you.

Leo Tolstoy

Slow down and enjoy life. It's not only
the scenery you miss by going too fast—you also miss
the sense of where you're going and why.

Eddie Cantor

One of the benefits that comes from slowing down our lives
is that it gives us the opportunity to get back in touch with
who we really are and what we're doing here.

Elaine St. James

There is more to life than increasing its speed.

Mahatma Gandhi

There's a lot we can do in the fast lane—we can grow
and we can expand. But we cannot deepen, and we cannot
integrate our experiences, unless we slow down.

Angeles Arrien

When we get too caught up in the busyness of the world,
we lose connection with one another—and ourselves.

Jack Kornfield

You can come to understand your
purpose in life by slowing down
and feeling your heart's desires.

Marcia Wieder

When we lack proper time for the simple pleasures of life,
for the enjoyment of eating, drinking, playing, creating,
visiting friends, and watching children at play,
then we have missed the purpose of life.

Ed Hayes

As technology continues to speed up our lives, we become
more and more stressed because we are unable physically
to go as fast as our machines would allow. Yet, we try
and try to keep up, only to fall further behind.

Lois Levy

I think God's going to come down
and pull civilization over for speeding.

Steven Wright

Just as your car runs more smoothly and requires less energy
to go faster and farther when the wheels
are in perfect alignment,
you perform better when your thoughts, feelings,
emotions, goals, and values are in balance.

Brian Tracy

Live a balanced life—learn some and think some and draw
and paint and sing and dance and play
and work every day some.

Robert Fulghum

Balance is the perfect state of still water. Let that be our model.
It remains quiet within and is not disturbed on the surface.

Confucius

Most men pursue pleasure with such breathless haste
they hurry past it.

Søren Kierkegaard

Whoever is in a hurry shows that the thing he is about
is too big for him.

Philip Dormer Stanhope

Slow down and everything you are chasing
will come around and catch you.

John de Paola

Have patience. Everything is difficult before it is easy.

Saadi

Be patient.
You'll know what it's time for you to wake up and move ahead.

Ram Dass

It is important from time to time to slow down,
to go away by yourself, and simply be.

Eileen Caddy

Life is all about timing.... The unreachable becomes reachable,
the unavailable become available, the unattainable...attainable.
Have the patience, wait it out. It's all about timing.

Stacey Charter

If they try to rush me, I always say,
"I've only got one other speed—and it's slower."

Glenn Ford

Hurrying up and using a lot of shortcuts
doesn't get us very far at all.

Fred Rogers

Her life was like running on a treadmill or riding on
a stationary bike; it was aerobic, it was healthy,
but she wasn't going anywhere.

Julia Phillips

Have patience! In time, even grass becomes milk.

Charan Singh

Learn the art of patience. Apply discipline to your thoughts
when they become anxious over the
outcome of a goal. Impatience
breeds anxiety, fear, discouragement
and failure. Patience creates
confidence, decisiveness and a rational outlook,
which eventually leads to success.

Brian Adams

Patience is the companion of wisdom.

Saint Augustine

There are three secrets to managing.
The first secret is to have patience. The second is to be patient.
And the third most important secret is patience.

Chuck Tanner

The key to everything is patience.
You get the chicken by hatching the egg, not by smashing it.

Arnold H. Glasgow

Have patience with all things, But, first of all with yourself.

Saint Francis de Sales

If you are patient in one moment of anger,
you will escape a hundred days of sorrow.

Chinese proverb

Adopt the pace of nature; her secret is patience.

Ralph Waldo Emerson

The trees that are slow to grow bear the best fruit.

Molière

Nature always takes her time.
Great oaks don't become great overnight.

Andrew Matthews

With time and patience the mulberry leaf becomes a silk gown.

Chinese proverb

Everything that slows us down and
forces patience, everything that
sets us back into the slow circles of nature, is a help.

May Sarton

Life is not a race, so take it slower,
hear the music before the song is over.

David L. Weatherford

Death is nature's way of telling you to slow down.

Anonymous

For fast acting relief, try slowing down.

Lily Tomlin

Take a Break

I have many apps on my cell phone. One of my favorites is also one of the simplest. It allows me to set a chime that rings at set intervals.

The reason I like this app is because a gentle "singing bowl" sound goes off every hour on the hour. It is a reminder to take a break, to stop whatever I'm doing, to take a couple of deep breaths, and perhaps to meditate. Sometimes I'll stop for only a minute or two, other times maybe five or ten minutes in order to get a snack, a cup of tea, or simply a walk around my office.

What is important is not how long the break is, or what it consists of, but that I take one. It helps me refresh. It helps me center myself. It helps me energize again before I go back to work. And since I do a lot of writing, it often gets my stagnated creative juices flowing again.

Most of us think that taking a break is a waste of time, that we will be less productive. But, according to scientific studies, we actually get more done because, among other things, our minds go numb when we focus on one thing for too long.

If you want to up your productivity and enjoyment of what you do, then build some downtime in your day. Follow the advice of the researchers, as well as the wise words from folks in this section, and take regular time-outs.

There is no trouble so great or grave
that cannot be much diminished by a nice cup of tea.

Bernard-Paul Heroux

The spirit of the tea beverage is one of peace,
comfort and refinement.

Arthur Gray

Tea was such a comfort.

Edna St. Vincent Millay

Tea and books—Mmmmmm, two of life's exquisite pleasures
that together bring near-bliss.

Christine Hanrahan

China tea, the scent of hyacinths, wood fires and bowls
of violets—that is my mental picture of an agreeable
February afternoon.

Constance Spry

Thank God for tea! What would the world do without tea?
How did it exist? I am glad I was not born before tea.

Sydney Smith

Take rest; a field that has rested gives a bountiful crop.

Ovid

Tea pot is on, the cups are waiting,
favorite chairs anticipating,
no matter what I have to do,
my friend there's always time for you.

Anonymous

We spend most of our time and energy in a kind of horizontal
thinking. We move along the surface of things... [but] there are
times when we stop. We sit still. We lose
ourselves in a pile of leaves
or its memory. We listen and breezes from a whole other
world begin to whisper.

James Carroll

A day out-of-doors, someone I love to
talk with, a good book and
some simple food and music—that would be rest.

Eleanor Roosevelt

All the trouble in the world is due to the fact
that man cannot sit still in a room.

Blaise Pascal

One must be out-of-doors enough to get experience
of wholesome reality, as a ballast to thought and sentiment.
Health requires this relaxation, this aimless life.

Henry David Thoreau

To sit in the shade on a fine day, and look upon
verdure, is the most perfect refreshment.

Jane Austen

If you get gloomy, just take an hour off
and sit and think how much
better this world is than hell. Of course, it won't cheer you up
if you expect to go there.

Don Marquis

If you are losing your leisure, look out;
you may be losing your soul.

Logan Pearsall Smith

It is in his pleasure that a man really lives; it is from his leisure
that he constructs the true fabric of self.

Agnes Repplier

Leisure is a form of silence, not noiselessness. It is the silence of contemplation such as occurs when we let our minds rest on a rosebud, a child at play, a Divine mystery, or a waterfall.

Fulton J. Sheen

Downtime is where we become ourselves, looking into the middle distance, kicking at the curb, lying on the grass or sitting on the stoop and staring at the tedious blue of the summer sky. I don't believe you can write poetry, or compose music, or become an actor without downtime, and plenty of it, a hiatus that passes for boredom but is really the quiet moving of the wheels inside that fuel creativity.

Anna Quindlen

People would have more leisure time if it weren't for all the leisure-time activities that use it up.

Peg Bracken

To be able to fill leisure intelligently is the last product of civilization, and at present very few people have reached this level.

Bertrand Russell

This art of resting the mind and the power of dismissing from it
all care and worry is probably one of the secrets of energy
in our great men.

J. A. Hadfield

A violin cannot play a sweet note unless the strings are
under pressure. But if you put too much pressure on the strings,
they snap. So do we. When the violin
is not being used, you release
the tension on the strings. We, too, need periods of relaxation
to recover and renew.

Tanya Wheway

Tension is who you think you should be.
Relaxation is who you are.

Chinese proverb

Distract your mind when you're under pressure.
Do something frivolous, nonstressful and unrelated to
"real life." Watch an old movie on TV, play with your dog,
do a crossword puzzle, take a long swim.

Sharon Gold

How beautiful it is to do nothing, and then rest afterward.

Spanish proverb

No matter how much pressure you feel
at work, if you could find
ways to relax for at least five minutes every hour,
you'd be more productive.

Joyce Brothers

Every now and then go away, have a
little relaxation, for when you
come back to your work your judgment
will be surer. Go some distance
away because then the work appears smaller and more of it
can be taken in at a glance and a lack of
harmony and proportion is
more readily seen.

Leonardo da Vinci

If a man insisted always on being serious, and never allowed
himself a bit of fun and relaxation, he would go mad
or become unstable without knowing it.

Herodotus

What I dream of is an art of balance, of purity and serenity
devoid of troubling or depressing subject matter—a soothing,
calming influence on the mind, rather like a good armchair
which provides relaxation from physical fatigue.

Henri Matisse

During [these] periods of relaxation
after concentrated intellectual
activity, the intuitive mind seems to
take over and can produce the
sudden clarifying insights which give so much joy and delight.

Fritjof Capra

It is better to have loafed and lost
than never to have loafed at all.

James Thurber

No day is so bad it can't be fixed with a nap.

Carrie Snow

I usually take a two-hour nap from one to four.

Yogi Berra

There is more refreshment and stimulation in a nap, even of the
briefest, than in all the alcohol ever distilled.

Ovid

It is well to lie fallow for a while.

Martin Farquhar Tupper

Think what a better world it would be if we all, the whole world,
had cookies and milk about three o'clock every afternoon
and then lay down on our blankets for a nap.

Barbara Jordan

Stress is an ignorant state. It believes that
everything is an emergency.
Nothing is that important. Just lie down.

Natalie Goldberg

Lie down and listen to the crabgrass grow,
the faucet leak, and learn to leave them so.

Marya Mannes

Learn to pause...or nothing worthwhile will catch up to you.

Doug King

Learning to ignore things is one of the
great paths to inner peace.

Robert J. Sawyer

There must be quite a few things a hot bath won't cure,
but I don't know many of them.

Sylvia Plath

A vacation is what you take when you can no longer
take what you've been taking.

Earl Wilson

You must have been warned against
letting the golden hours slip by.
Yes, but some of them are golden only because we let them slip.

J. M. Barrie

The time to relax is when you don't have time for it.

Sydney J. Harris

Closing Thought

> Simplicity is making the journey of this life with just baggage enough.
>
> ***Charles Dudley Warner***

Dear Reader

Thank you so much for reading my book. I am honored that out of the thousands of books published each year, you have chosen to spend some time with this one.

As in all my writing, my goal is to help you have a richer and more enjoyable life. If you get just one thing from this book that helps you do that, then all the many hours I spent putting this book together has been worth it.

Writing is a lonely business. Authors spend months, sometimes years, completing a book. Then, if they are lucky, their work gets published. The book is birthed into the world and they never know how it may have influenced a reader. It would therefore be thrilling to hear your response after reading *The Joy of Simplicity*. My email address is allen@allenklein.com

I would also love to have you post a review on Amazon: www.amazon.com/Joy-Simplicity-Insights-Unclutter-Uncomplicate/dp/164250145X/

Thanks a bundle,

ALLEN

P.S. To show my appreciation for your support of my work, I'd like to send you an article I wrote titled "Three Questions You Need to Ask Yourself If You Want More Joy in Your Life." To get it, email me at allen@allenklein.com.

Index

D

E

F

G

H

L

M

About the Author

Allen Klein is an award-winning professional keynote speaker and bestselling author. He is a recipient of a Lifetime Achievement Award from the Association for Applied and Therapeutic Humor, a Certified Speaking Professional designation from the National Speakers Association, a Communication and Leadership Award from Toastmasters International, and an inductee in the Hunter Hall of Fame at Hunter College, New York City.

Klein is also the author of thirty books including *The Healing Power of Humor*, *You Can't Ruin My Day*, *Embracing Life After Loss*, *Positive Thoughts for Troubling Times*, and *The Lighten Up Book*. In addition, he is a TEDx presenter on the power of intention. Klein's TEDx talk is available online: www.youtube.com/watch?v=rqPu52vWpJA&t=7s

For more information about Klein's books or presentations, go to www.allenklein.com or contact him at allen@allenklein.com.

mango PUBLISHING

Mango Publishing, established in 2014, publishes an eclectic list of books by diverse authors–both new and established voices–on topics ranging from business, personal growth, women's empowerment, LGBTQ studies, health, and spirituality to history, popular culture, time management, decluttering, lifestyle, mental wellness, aging, and sustainable living. We were recently named 2019's #1 fastest growing independent publisher by Publishers Weekly. Our success is driven by our main goal, which is to publish high quality books that will entertain readers as well as make a positive difference in their lives.

Our readers are our most important resource; we value your input, suggestions, and ideas. We'd love to hear from you–after all, we are publishing books for you!

Please stay in touch with us and follow us at:

Facebook: Mango Publishing
Twitter: @MangoPublishing
Instagram: @MangoPublishing
LinkedIn: Mango Publishing
Pinterest: Mango Publishing

Sign up for our newsletter at www.mangopublishinggroup.com and receive a free book!

Join us on Mango's journey to reinvent publishing, one book at a time.